10-19

# INSIDE THE NSA

**Chris Townsend**

**Enslow Publishing**
101 W. 23rd Street
Suite 240
New York, NY 10011
USA

enslow.com

Published in 2020 by Enslow Publishing, LLC
101 W. 23rd Street, Suite 240, New York, NY 10011

**Library of Congress Cataloging-in-Publication Data**

Names: Townsend, Chris, author.
Title: Inside the NSA / Chris Townsend.
Description: New York : Enslow Publishing, 2020. | Series: Inside law enforcement | Includes bibliographical references and index. | Audience: Grade 5 to 8.
Identifiers: LCCN 2018058105| ISBN 9781978507364 (library bound) | ISBN 9781978508576 (pbk.)
Subjects: LCSH: United States. National Security Agency/Central Security Service—Juvenile literature. | Intelligence service—United States—Juvenile literature.
Classification: LCC JK468.I6 T655 2020 | DDC 327.1273—dc23
LC record available at https://lccn.loc.gov/2018058105

Printed in the United States of America

**To Our Readers:** We have done our best to make sure all website addresses in this book were active and appropriate when we went to press. However, the author and the publisher have no control over and assume no liability for the material available on those website or on any website they may link to. Any comments or suggestions can be sent by email to customerservice@enslow.com.

**Photo Credits:** Cover, pp. 1, 32 Brooks Kraft/Corbis/Getty Images; p. 5 Greg Mathieson/Mai/The LIFE Images Collection/Getty Images; p. 8 tantawat/Shutterstock.com; p. 11 Tim Page/Corbis Historical/Getty Images; p. 14 Ivan Cholakov/Shutterstock.com; pp. 17, 39 The Washington Post/Getty Images; p. 18 AFP/Getty Images; p. 21 Nirat.pix/Shutterstock.com; p. 22 Everett Historical/Shutterstock.com; p. 26 Science & Society Picture Library/Getty Images; p. 28 Bettmann/Getty Images; p. 29 vchal/Shutterstock.com; p. 34 Bro Crock/Shutterstock.com; p. 35 Adam Berry/Getty Images; p. 40 Osabee/Shutterstock.com.

# CONTENTS

# INTRODUCTION

The United States created the National Security Agency (NSA) almost seventy years ago. It was founded in secrecy. Even the existence of the agency was a secret! Most Americans never even knew about the NSA until years later. The NSA has had many nicknames over the years, like "No Such Agency" and the "Puzzle Palace."

The NSA has been in the news a lot recently. No longer secret, the NSA is now a visible part of our government and security. Former directors even write opinion pieces for major newspapers about their service.[1] But what does the NSA do behind closed doors?

The mission of the NSA includes intelligence, cryptology, and cyber-security. The type of intelligence the NSA deals with is called signals intelligence. It is usually just referred to as SIGINT for short. Cryptology is all about making and cracking codes. Finally, the NSA is responsible for cybersecurity. It keeps the computer networks safe. It also protects the information on those networks.

In this book, we will go inside the NSA. We'll look at how these smart women and men keep us safe. Every day, thousands of people go to work around the country. Their mission is to gather information, crack codes, and protect networks.

The NSA has a short but storied history, and this book will explore all the different things the agency has done, from the early days of technology-based spying and intelligence gathering to its work after September 11,

While the work the National Security Agency (NSA) does is kept secret, its existence is well known because of the many controversies the agency has faced over the years.

2001, to everything since in the name of protecting the country from future terror attacks.

The NSA is not the only intelligence agency in the United States. It must work with the other US intelligence agencies and even agencies around the world. There is a lot of information floating around us in the air or zipping around in lines all around us. The NSA's job is to look at suspicious transmissions and warn us if there is danger. There are some codes so complex that they have never been broken!

The NSA also protects against people trying to get into our computer systems to change our messages or to stop us from collecting their messages. Hackers are always trying to get into networks. Some want to steal information. Others just want to break stuff and cause trouble. The NSA has to defend the networks. It also ensures that the information traveling on networks is secure and correct.

However, even with all of this information, it is still a secret exactly how many people work for the NSA. Most guess that thirty thousand to forty thousand people work for the agency, but no one outside the agency knows for sure. All we can know is that a diverse, skilled group of people from all backgrounds and specialties work to keep us and our government's networks safe.

# CHAPTER 1

# SHROUDED IN SECRETS

Before the NSA existed, there were a number of other agencies that looked for intelligence. For a while, the US Army led the effort to collect and use intelligence. President Harry S. Truman created the NSA as a government agency in 1952. In 1975, the bubble of secrecy was broken as the NSA was brought before Congress to explain itself. The testimony shocked Americans. Congress created a new law. It forbids the NSA from spying on American citizens. After the United States was attacked on September 11, 2001, the NSA once again began growing. Its mission today is more important than ever.

## Born in the Shadows

In January 1917, the world was at war. Germany had declared war on Russia and France in 1914. Britain then declared war on Germany. Turkey joined with the Germans. Americans watched the war from afar for three years. Even after a German submarine, called a U-boat, sank an American cruise ship, the United States stayed out of the fight. A single telegram changed everything.

British intelligence captured a telegram from Germany to Mexico. The telegram was filled with nothing but numbers. The British realized it was a coded message. They cracked the code. The message from the Germans asked Mexico to attack the United States! If the United States was fighting its neighbor, it would likely stay out of the fight in Europe. Germany promised Mexico land in America as a reward.

In the earliest days of US intelligence gathering, agents passed messages through coded telegraphs, using Morse code to convey their secrets back and forth.

The Zimmerman Telegram, as it came to be known, showed America that it could not stay out of the fight. In April 1917, it declared war on Germany. The importance of intercepting and decoding enemy messages was clear. America needed its own code breakers.

In July 1917, it created the Cipher Bureau. For twelve years, the bureau collected intelligence, including every telegram entering the United States from abroad. The army took over intelligence in 1929. In 1942, the army cracked Japan's secret code. The cracked code allowed the United States to predict a Japanese attack at Midway in the Pacific Ocean. Later, another intercept allowed the United States to shoot down a plane carrying the leader of the Japanese military.[1]

## In from the Cold

After World War II, the United States set up the National Security Agency. By 1969, it was the largest intelligence agency in the country and maybe the whole world![2] The relationship between the United States and the Soviet Union fell apart after their alliance during World War II. For decades, the United States and the Soviet Union spied on each other during what became known as the Cold War. The Cold War wasn't always cold. Hot spots flared up in places like Germany, Cuba, and East Asia.

The NSA put antennae all over the world to listen in on Soviet information. Ships, planes, and satellites deep in space circled the globe constantly looking for any sign of danger to the United States. In 1962, the NSA saw that the Soviets were putting nuclear missiles in Cuba. Cuba is only 90 miles (145 kilometers) from the United States. Without the NSA the United States might never have known that it was in danger. After a tense standoff, the Soviet Union finally removed the nuclear missiles.

On August 2, 1964, a US Navy ship was collecting intelligence near the Gulf of Tonkin. North Vietnamese boats shot at the ship. Two nights later, two ships returned and were again attacked! The NSA confirmed the attacks. Soon, the United States was at war in Vietnam. There's just one small problem. In 2001, the NSA admitted that the second attack never happened.[3] It was a deliberate lie. The United States spent over ten years in a war that cost more than a million lives.

## A New Era

With all the negative attention, the budget and staff of the NSA shrank. The NSA continued to listen quietly in the background, but the new law meant it could only listen to foreign communications. Even so, at the end of the twentieth century, the world was beginning to go digital and talking more and more by computer and cell phone. There was so much information out there that it became difficult to monitor it all.

Then on September 11, 2001, terrorists attacked the United States. After the attacks, people wanted to know why the United States didn't

## A CAUSE FOR WAR

In 1975, Congress discovered that the NSA existed. It realized the NSA was getting more money than the intelligence agency Congress had established, the Central Intelligence Agency (CIA). Senator Frank Church set up a committee. It found out that the NSA had been spying on Americans through intercepted telegrams and other means for more than thirty years! Well-known Americans like actress Jane Fonda and Martin Luther King Jr. were the subjects of NSA spying.[4] Surprised and angry, the senators passed a new law forbidding the NSA from spying on Americans.

In the 1970s, US involvement in the Vietnam War was considered extremely controversial, and the NSA was partially responsible for America's long stay in the country.

know that the attacks was coming. The NSA, CIA, and FBI all had pieces of information. The problem found by the commission investigating the attacks was that none of the agencies talked much to one another.

The NSA was given strong new powers that allowed it to listen in on a wide variety of communications. From intercepting emails and phone calls to even tapping fiber optic cables on the ocean floor, the NSA had ears everywhere. Secret warrants once again allowed spying on Americans.[5] In 2013, many of these programs were exposed by a former worker.

The future of the NSA remains to be seen. Once again, its activities have been cut back. President Barack Obama promised that the NSA would not keep information on any American emails or phone calls that were collected by accident. The NSA is still very important to our security. Most of the information briefed to the president every morning comes from the NSA.[6]

# CHAPTER 2

# A PLACE AT THE TABLE

The NSA is actually part of the Department of Defense. Most people think of the armed forces when they think of the Department of Defense. The NSA is one of many intelligence agencies in the United States. The NSA focuses on collecting signals from foreign countries in the agency's efforts to defend our country. But the NSA is not the only one listening. Around the world, most developed countries have an agency responsible for listening for trouble. The NSA is part of a broad effort in the United States and around that world. Every day, it looks for needles in digital haystacks to keep us safe.

## Light in the Dark

The NSA was established in 1952 as part of the Department of Defense. This made sense at the time because the US Army was responsible for most of the country's intelligence collection. The NSA defends the

United States by listening in to communications from around the world. It also collects and reads messages sent by email or text message. Since 1975, the NSA has been ordered to keep its ears facing outward.

Since 1972, the NSA has partnered with intelligence agencies in the other military services, like the Marine Corps and the Navy, through the Central Security Service (CSS).[1] The military is deployed all over the world. This means it can often intercept signals that would otherwise be missed. Nearly every country hides important or sensitive information by using codes. The CSS manages the military's coding efforts. It makes

The NSA doesn't work alone. While it handles many intelligence-gathering activities solo, it also partners with other US agencies to provide the government with the most thorough information.

sure that the United States has a smart strategy for intercepting and using signals.

The NSA is like a giant tape recorder that captures all kinds of information from around the world. It uses this information to try to keep the United States safe. When it finds a threat in the information, it works with other agencies or through the military to address those threats. Keeping the country's ears open through agencies like the NSA will hopefully prevent attacks from foreign actors outside the United States that seek to do the United States harm. Of course, the NSA is not alone in this effort. The NSA partners with many of the other intelligence agencies. These agencies work in the United States and all over the world.

## One of Many

The NSA is very specialized. It focuses on intercepting signals and decoding them. It also makes sure US information is safe from prying eyes. Because it is so specialized, the NSA cannot keep us safe all by itself. Not all threats can be discovered from just listening in and reading

### HOW MANY INTEL AGENCIES ARE THERE!?!

There are at least seventeen intelligence agencies in the United States.[2] There's the Director of National Intelligence. Most know the NSA, FBI, and CIA. Additionally, the State Department has intel offices. You also find intel offices in the Departments of Homeland Security, Treasury, and Energy, and in the DEA. On top of those, there are other agencies that collect information, like the National Geospatial-Intelligence Agency and National Reconnaissance Office. Each military service has its own intelligence branch. There are a lot of eyes and ears out there!

the bad guys' emails. Other agencies are each responsible for different parts of US security.

The FBI collects information from inside the United States about potential crimes. The CIA relies on human intelligence gathered by spies all over the world. The DEA looks at drug dealers and their criminal networks. The Department of Energy looks for threats to power plants and other infrastructure. The Department of the Treasury prevents threats to the financial system. Together, they make a giant net designed to keep any threat from slipping through.

An investigation after September 11, 2001, determined that one of the problems was that the different intelligence agencies were not good at talking to one another. They didn't like to share information. In the intel world, information is power. The United States created a new office for a Director of National Intelligence to try and improve the information sharing. By combining the foreign intelligence from the NSA with other types of information from the other agencies, the DNI can make sure the United States has a clear picture of any threats.

## Around the World

The United States and the National Security Agency are not alone in listening in. After all, it was the British who intercepted and decoded the Zimmerman Telegram before the United States even had a signals intelligence agency. Improving technology meant communication was no longer limited to word of mouth or letters. With the rise of phones, radios, and computers, many of the world's governments took steps to keep their people safe. In 2013, an NSA employee revealed that the NSA had actually been spying on many of America's friends in addition to its enemies.

Because terrorism is a global threat, many nations share information with each other to try and stop attacks before they happen. According

Heads of the FBI, CIA, and National Intelligence (pictured), along with the head of the NSA, testified before Congress in February 2018 on threats to the US elections from Russia.

to British newspapers, the British Government Communications Headquarters and German Foreign Intelligence Service have shared "massive amounts" of information with the NSA.[3]

The international intelligence agencies are like an alphabet soup of letters and acronyms. Because they are often foreign acronyms, the

One of the main jobs of the NSA is to help monitor communications between suspected terrorists from around the world who may wish to harm Americans.

abbreviations of foreign intelligence agencies are almost like a code! Other countries that work with the NSA include Australia, Canada, Denmark, France, Israel, Italy, the Netherlands, Norway, Spain, and Switzerland. Global security is a group effort!

Of course, not only friendly nations are listening in. For decades, the Russian KGB carried out activities to collect information inside and outside the Soviet Union. Today, the Chinese, North Koreans, and Iranians have also turned their ears toward the world.[4] Some of these countries use their surveillance efforts to steal secrets about businesses all over the world.

# CHAPTER 3

# THE WALLS HAVE EARS

Since the beginning, the main mission of the NSA has been the collection of information. Like a giant vacuum cleaner, the NSA sucks up intelligence from all over the world. Communications were simpler when the agency was founded. Now the agency has to deal with many different means of communicating. Radios, telephone calls, emails, text messages, chat applications, and even video game chats represent sources of information. Collecting the information is only half the challenge. Once the NSA has the data, it has to see if there is anything important. It's like looking for a needle in a haystack on a massive scale.

## Listening In

In the early days, the NSA focused on radio signals and telegrams. The first target of the NSA was the Soviet Union. The NSA surrounded the Soviets with radio towers that were 100 feet (30 meters) tall and 1,000 feet (305 m) wide.[1] There was no signal the Soviets could send that could not be heard by these massive antennae. Of course, the Soviets knew the United States was listening and made sure to use codes to hide their messages!

In addition to all the antennae around the world, the NSA had access to the military services. Twenty-four hours a day and seven days a week, American ships and planes went about their business all over the world. Some planes and ships existed for the sole purpose of capturing intelligence. What began as picture taking became a significant ability to gather intelligence from all over the world.

With the advent of space travel, a new frontier opened up in the spy game. Soon, Earth was ringed with satellites. These devices take pictures of what's below them and intercept signals from the surface. The United States alone has thousands of these spy satellites orbiting Earth.[2] No one outside the government really knows the exact number of US spy satellites currently in orbit.

We know even less about what satellites other countries have put into space or what they may be capable of. You can look at the night sky on any clear night, and if you wait long enough you will see quick blinking lights pass overhead. It is one of many satellites spinning around the globe.

## SIGINT

The military uses many types of intelligence. HUMINT is intelligence collected from humans. IMINT is intelligence from pictures. MASINT is intelligence about radar signs. OSINT uses open sources like newspapers and the internet. GEOINT relies on maps.[3] The type of intelligence that is most important to the NSA is signals intelligence, or SIGINT.

SIGINT involves the collection of signals. They can be physical or electronic. Communications, electronic emissions, and any signal from a

While we think of intelligence as being messages on paper that can be filed, it actually comes in many forms, such as maps, messages, newspapers, interviews with people, and computer data.

foreign country can be a source of SIGINT. Since its earliest iterations, the NSA has collected signals from all over the world. It hopes to study these signals and learn about any threats.

In 1894, a German scientist found invisible waves in the air. An Italian, Guglielmo Marconi, figured out how to make these waves. His first device could send signals for a mile. Then, he sent a signal across the ocean.[4] Soon, radios and more sophisticated machines were sending invisible messages through the air. It wasn't long before countries began to intercept each other's communications during

Radio waves can carry messages meant for the public, like you hear on the radio, but they can also carry hidden messages heard only by those who know exactly which frequency to listen to.

conflict. Once computers and computer networks spanned the globe, the amount of information grew.

SIGINT is all about intercepting and making use of the information all around us, seen and unseen. Today's methods are very sophisticated. Any type of information out there right now can be intercepted. Eventually, quantum technology could make SIGINT impossible, as it could eliminate the computer networks that hold onto messages and make interception possible. Quantum computers will eventually reduce communications security to a physical security problem. These advanced computers could also crack any code you could devise.

## Too Close to Home?

The NSA was formed to keep an ear on the world. It is impossible to be listening to everything and not come across some information you're not supposed to hear. After finding out the NSA had spied on American citizens since 1945, Congress prevented the agency from spying on Americans in 1975. The terror attacks in 2001 led to new laws that allowed the government to listen in on American residents and citizens in the name of homeland security. But it wasn't long until it was discovered that the NSA may have listened to more than it should have under these new laws. An NSA employee, Edward Snowden, went public with many of the programs on which he worked that directly or indirectly spied on Americans.

### EDWARD SNOWDEN

Depending on whom you ask, Edward Snowden is either a traitor or a hero. In 2013, he fled to Hong Kong after downloading thousands of secret files that showed the US government had indeed spied on Americans. The programs responsible for spying on Americans had collected data from cell phone companies and the internet. Additionally, Snowden revealed that the United States had also spied on its friends. Snowden then fled to Russia, where he currently lives. If he returns to the United States, he will be prosecuted. He broke the law by stealing all those secret files.

Many Americans were scared after the attacks on September 11, 2001. The government created broad new powers to collect information. Secret warrants were issued that allowed the government to collect information even on American citizens. All it took was convincing a judge that a potential threat existed.

After Edward Snowden, the government was forced to admit that it had collected, stored, and used more information than anyone realized. Beyond just phone calls, massive amounts of information on people's internet browsing and other online activities found their way into government databases. The incident led to President Obama promising that no more information about Americans would be stored on government networks.[5] Communications from overseas were still fair game. Any American talking to or from a person in a foreign country could still be recorded.

# CHAPTER 4

# CRACKING THE CODE

Writing things down is a great way to remember them. Information can easily be sent from one person to another. But what if you want to keep the information secret? What if you only want a certain person to read it? Cryptology is the study of codes or ciphers. Ciphers are a system of writing that disguises what is actually being said. For thousands of years, people have hidden messages in various codes. Today, computers can make very hard codes. The NSA has been making and breaking codes since it began. It keeps information safe by hiding it in plain sight!

## Hidden Messages

Before codes, people would use all sorts of ways to hide messages. Writing on a paper with lemon juice leaves invisible words on the page until the page is heated. The words will appear like magic! According to the ancient

The Enigma cypher machine (*above*) was used by Germans in World War II to encode secret messages and share them only with their allies, who knew how to crack the code.

historian Herodotus, one king sent a messenger to another country. When the messenger arrived, he gave the other king his message. "Shave my head," he said. The secret message had been tattooed on the messenger's head months earlier! When his hair grew back it hid the message.[1]

The oldest known use of a cypher to hide valuable information was over 3,500 years ago.[2] A potter in ancient Iraq wanted to write down the formula for his glazing method. To hide his secret, he used a phonetic version of cuneiform, an early writing system.

As writing spread, so did many other forms of encoding messages. Sensitive commercial, military, or political messages were encrypted. By the time the NSA came along, codes had been used for thousands of years. In the early days of the NSA, messages were captured from radio and telegram transmissions. Cracking the code meant figuring out what the messages actually said.

With the advent of computers, it became very difficult to break messages. Computers allowed for very complicated codes based on math. Without the original formula or algorithm used to mix up a message, it is nearly impossible to figure it out. Someday soon, quantum computers could make code breaking obsolete. They could crack any code we could devise very quickly.

## A=1, B=2 ...

One of the simplest types of cryptography is a substitution code. In a substitution code, the letters or numbers in a message are the result of

### MAKE YOUR OWN SECRET CODE

Want to make a secret code to send messages to your friends? Write the letters A through Z down one side of a piece of paper. Now choose a random letter somewhere down the list. Beside that letter start writing A through Z again. When you reach Z, you'll have to start the list at A again until you reach the end of your first list. You might end up with R=A, S=B, and so on. R=A is the key. Once you know that, you can write and break the code. Give your friends the key, or hide it in the message and you are all set!

putting the original message through a cypher. A simple version of this cypher substitutes a number for a letter of the alphabet. If A=1 and B=2, and so on until Z=26, then a string of numbers can actually be a word. "Cat" could be spelled 3-1-20. More complicated systems like the one used in the Zimmerman Telegram substitute a string of numbers for an entire word or phrase.

Before computers and encrypted radios, most of the codes that the NSA had to crack were variations of these substitution codes. If it could figure out the substitution method, it could crack any message sent using

Not all codes can be cracked by computers. Below are the notes of a Russian spy who kept track of information the old-fashioned way: with a pen and paper.

that code. Eventually, mechanical coders like special typewriters made messages that were too hard for people to figure out. There were just too many combinations until computers came along.

Today, the NSA relies on very sophisticated computers and encryption devices. These devices scramble a message by mixing in a separate signal or using math. Unless you have the signal or formula that is mixed in, you have no way to tell what the real message is and what is noise. Since these noise patterns are created by computers, they are impossible for a person to break without help.

## Safe from Prying Eyes

Most of the NSA's encryption and decryption methods are secret. After all, it is trying to protect information. If its codes and methods got out, our enemies would know all of our secrets. Most of the United States' codes today are based on very complicated math problems. The math problems often rely on prime numbers. Prime numbers are those that can only be divided by one and themselves.

It is simple to take two or more prime numbers and multiply them together. It is very difficult to go in the other direction. If you start with a very large number and try to sort out the original prime numbers used to make it, even a computer may take years to figure it out. Even though people know how to break these codes, we just don't have enough brain or computer power to actually do it!

The NSA uses a lot of different types of encryption. More important or secret information is coded with harder methods to crack. The NSA provides many of its codes for use. But the NSA has warned businesses that the cryptology world may be changing.

Soon, quantum computers may make encryption useless. Quantum computers can do math so fast that no current code can stay secret for long. To stay ahead of the fight, the NSA is working to develop a new set of codes that even quantum computers can't break.[3]

# CHAPTER 5

# DEFENDING THE NETWORK

The third of the NSA's primary missions is information assurance. Today, we usually just call it cybersecurity. Cybersecurity is all about securing machines and information that are connected to and shared via our various computer networks. We know already that the NSA is always listening all over the world. Of course, others want to listen to US information, too. Economic secrets can be worth big money. Some countries want to steal that information instead of researching for themselves. Enemies also may want to know what the military is doing or what world leaders are saying to one another. Part of the NSA's mission is protecting US information.

## World Wide Web

Today, the computer on your desk and the phone in your hand are connected to every other device on the network. That network spans the entire planet! If you are on the internet, you are connected to every other device on the internet. Because everything is connected, everything is subject to hacking. In some homes, even refrigerators and doorbells are on the internet chatting away with the world. Without security on these devices, anyone can talk to them or take information from them.

All these connections are both good and bad for the NSA. It can use the connections to get information. It can also be attacked from any direction. This means it is constantly on guard. It has to watch for intruders. Even before an attacker strikes, the NSA is working to make the information and the network more secure. It's like putting something

Agents of the NSA are working constantly to defend the US government from cyber attacks by hackers who want to access our information or secrets.

special to you in a safe, then putting that safe in a vault, then locking the door to the building the vault is in.

To help the United States and the world keep the internet safe, the NSA is responsible for keeping networks secure. Some secret networks are totally separate from the rest of the internet. The NSA knows so much about cybersecurity that it actually sets the standards that the rest of the world follows.[2] It provides lists of best practices for securing networks and information. It also puts out warnings when it sees danger.

## White Hat Hacking

Most people think of hackers as bad guys. They sneak into networks and steal information. They break people's computers. They work for their own profit or for a shady company or evil government. The same skills that can be used for evil in the world can be used to protect us from danger! The NSA relies on very smart people who are just as good as the bad hackers. Sometimes, these hackers are referred to as white hat

## THE FIRST HACK

Guglielmo Marconi invented the wireless telegraph, completing his first wireless telegraph transmission in 1897. For the first time, messages could be sent invisibly through the air. Marconi was also the very first person to get hacked! Marconi had gathered many important people to demonstrate his new invention. He had invented a wireless printer for his telegraph. It was not secure. As the men watched, the machine started spitting out the word "RATS" over and over![1] Another inventor had hijacked the machine and sent his own message.

Most information today is stored on computer servers like these. That's why the NSA works so hard to find and stop hackers, or people trying to illegally access the information stored on computers.

hackers because they are the good guys, and in traditional fairy tales, the good guys always wear white!

Like the cowboys from old western movies dueled in dusty streets, white hat hackers and black hat hackers face off across the network. Some white hat hackers are former black hats, so they know many of the tricks! The NSA hires people with college experience in programming or math, but it also hires people who are just really good with computers and networks. One former white hat hacker for the NSA noted that these good hackers can make from $40,000 to $240,000 a year![3]

The NSA is looking for the best. Sometimes, that means looking in strange places. In 2013, the director of the NSA went to a conference called Black Hat.[4] Many of the best hackers in the world attend this conference. The director's message was simple. He was asking for the hackers to help the United States protect its information and networks from the bad guys. After Edward Snowden, a lot of people don't trust the NSA. It's hard to get and keep good people if everyone thinks you are the bad guy!

## Tools of the Trade

The NSA has more information about computer networks and threats than anyone else because every single day it is watching and protecting the network. This gives it a good chance to help others understand the threats. The NSA has tried to be a force for good by sharing its infor-

Hacking has become such a popular activity that there are now hacker conventions and conferences held around the world. Some of these hackers end up working for the NSA.

mation and tools with others. People that want to use NSA encryption can apply for access. They can then build computers or other network devices that can use the best encryption the NSA has.

Aside from these encryption programs and protocols, the NSA uses a variety of tools and software to perform its job. Some of these programs have been challenged as too invasive. When you send information on the internet, it is usually split up and put into digital envelopes called packets. One NSA program could open these packets as they passed through the network. This allowed it to secretly read anything that was sent on the internet.[5]

Of course, its goal was to read the mail of bad people who want to do bad things, but it is impossible to not accidentally collect some information from the very people it was trying to protect. The Fourth Amendment to the US Constitution as written in the Bill of Rights forbids "unreasonable search." Because they capture information from people who are not suspected of a crime and without a warrant, some of these programs are being challenged in court.

# CHAPTER 6

# JOINING THE TEAM

The NSA needs the very best and brightest people to protect the United States and its information. Not everybody at the NSA is a hacker or computer programmer, though. Just like any other office, it takes a whole team of people working around the clock to do the job. The NSA also reaches out to students and offers many scholarships and grants. These outreach programs talk to college students and even kindergartners![1] One of the biggest needs in the NSA is for people who can speak foreign languages. After all, we can't always expect the bad guys to use English!

## Types of Jobs

The NSA lists seventeen different categories of jobs on its website.[2] Many of these jobs relate to the three core missions of the NSA: intelligence, cryptology, and cybersecurity. The NSA also needs people to answer the phones, pay the bills, and clean the buildings. Intelligence jobs include analysis, collection, and foreign languages. Cryptology jobs usually involve math and computers. Cybersecurity jobs also involve computers and math but also a good understanding of engineering and networks. It takes a lot of others to enable the people who work on the main missions of the NSA.

The NSA also hires people to do foreign language analysis. It needs people to run the business, like managing the budget. It has inspectors who ensure computers, software, and networks are secure. To make sure it stays on the right side of the law, the NSA hires lawyers and legal analysts. It also hires doctors, psychologists, and other medical professionals to work as consultants. Because its buildings are so secure, the NSA hires its own security and law enforcement.

You'll also find secretaries and human resources professionals inside the buildings. The NSA hires teachers and trainers to make sure its staff is as smart as possible. Because the NSA is funded through taxpayer money, it is important to communicate with people and the government about the mission. To do this, the NSA hires communications and public affairs workers. Finally, the NSA hires people to manage the logistics of its operations around the globe.

## CAN YOU PASS THE FIZZBUZZ TEST?

While the interview process is secret, some have talked about it on websites like Glassdoor.[3] One of the stranger parts of a test to be a hacker for the NSA is called the FizzBuzz test. Applicants are told to write a computer program that can count to 100. The program must replace any multiple of 3 with the word "Fizz." Any multiple of five must print out "Buzz." Multiples of both print out "FizzBuzz." A good programmer can write this program in only ten lines.

The NSA isn't only for people who are good with computers. It also hires people with other skills, like foreign languages, managing budgets, practicing law, or even running an office.

## How to Join

The NSA needs very reliable people to guard the nation's secrets. To ensure only the best get hired, the NSA has a few requirements. Workers must get a security clearance. To make sure workers are trustworthy, the NSA looks at their life history and record. Workers must be US citizens. Drugs are forbidden, even in states that legally allow marijuana. Finally, the agency looks at the integrity and medical fitness of applicants. Those who meet the eligibility requirements can apply to be interviewed. There are a few different steps in the interview process.

The first step is a review of qualifications and an initial interview. In addition to interviews, there is a psychological profile and even a lie detector test.[4] Part of the application process is to fill out a document for a background check. This document looks at the last ten years of the person's life. An investigator will take the form and check to make sure that the information is correct. They may even go and talk to people who know the applicant to find out what kind of person they are! People who meet the requirements and pass a background check and all the other tests are invited to join the team.

Getting a job with the NSA isn't easy, but anyone who wants to try is welcome to apply.

## Keeping Us Safe

The NSA does very important work. It needs the very best people to do it. These people must be very smart. They must also be very trustworthy. NSA workers handle some of the country's most secret information. They must not spy on Americans. Citizens have to be able to trust that if the NSA accidentally gets the information of regular Americans, it will discard it. Fortunately for us, there are thousands of Americans who have answered the call to serve. They work around the world and around the clock to protect us and our information.

Every day, the NSA is at work making and breaking codes. It collects information. It protects the networks and our own information. These three core missions and the people who carry them out protect us and keep us informed. Since 1952, the NSA has stood guard against the enemies of the United States. Whether we need them to intercept, analyze, or protect, the NSA is ready. Its mission is clear from its slogan: "Defending our Nation. Securing the Future."[5]

# CHAPTER NOTES

## Introduction

1. Michael Hayden, "The End of Intelligence," *New York Times*, April 28, 2018, https://www.nytimes.com/2018/04/28/opinion/sunday/the-end-of-intelligence.html.

## Chapter 1: Shrouded in Secrets

1. Michael X. Heiligenstein, "A Brief History of the NSA: From 1917 to 2014," *Saturday Evening Post*, April 17, 2014, https://www.saturdayevening-post.com/2014/04/a-brief-history-of-the-nsa.
2. Ibid.
3. Elisabeth Bumiller, "Records Show Doubts on '64 Vietnam Crisis," *New York Times*, July 14, 2010, https://www.nytimes.com/2010/07/15/world/asia/15vietnam.html.
4. Theunis Bates, "The Evolution of the NSA," *The Week,* February 5, 2014, https://theweek.com/articles/450898/evolution-nsa.
5. Heiligenstein, "A Brief History of the NSA."
6. Bates, "The Evolution of the NSA."

## Chapter 2: A Place at the Table

1. National Security Agency, "Central Security Service," https://www.nsa.gov/about/central-security-service.
2. Nina Agrawal, "There's More than the CIA and FBI: The 17 Agencies that Make up the U.S. Intelligence Community," *Los Angeles Times*, January 17, 2017, http://www.latimes.com/nation/la-na-17-intelligence-agencies-20170112-story.html.
3. Julian Borger, "GCHQ and European Spy Agencies Worked Together on Mass Surveillance," *Guardian*, November 1, 2013, https://www.

theguardian.com/uk-news/2013/nov/01/gchq-europe-spy-agencies-mass-surveillance-snowden.

4. United States Department of Defense, "Summary of the 2018 National Defense Strategy," https://dod.defense.gov/Portals/1/Documents/pubs/2018-National-Defense-Strategy-Summary.pdf.

## Chapter 3: The Walls Have Ears

1. Theunis Bates, "The Evolution of the NSA," *The Week,* February 5, 2014, https://theweek.com/articles/450898/evolution-nsa.

2. Geoff Manaugh, "Tracking Earth's Secret Spy Satellites," *Atlantic,* June 10, 2016, https://www.theatlantic.com/technology/archive/2016/06/mapping-clandestine-moons/485915.

3. ODNI, "What Is Intelligence?" https://www.dni.gov/index.php/what-we-do/what-is-intelligence.

4. History Channel, "Guglielmo Marconi," https://www.history.com/topics/inventions/guglielmo-marconi.

5. Michael X. Heiligenstein, "A Brief History of the NSA: From 1917 to 2014," *Saturday Evening Post*, April 17, 2014, https://www.saturdayevening-post.com/2014/04/a-brief-history-of-the-nsa.

## Chapter 4: Cracking the Code

1. Herodotus, *The Persian War,* The Modern Library, 1942, http://mcad-ams.posc.mu.edu/txt/ah/Herodotus/Herodotus7.html.

2. David Kahn, *The Codebreakers: A Comprehensive History of Secret Communication from Ancient Times to the Internet* (New York, NY: Scribner, 1996).

3. Dan Goodin, "NSA Preps Quantum-Resistant Algorithms to Head off Crypto-Apocalypse," *Ars Technica,* https://arstechnica.com/information-technology/2015/08/nsa-preps-quantum-resistant-algorithms-to-head-off-crypto-apocolypse.

## Chapter 5: Defending the Network

1. Alexis C. Madrigal, "The Great Wireless Hack of 1903," *The Atlantic,* December 29, 2011, https://www.theatlantic.com/technology/archive/2011/12/the-great-wireless-hack-of-1903/250665.
2. NSA, "What Is the NSA's Role in U.S. Cybersecurity?" https://www.nsa.gov/what-we-do/cybersecurity.
3. Ester Bloom, "What This ex-NSA Agent wants You to Know About Your Smartphone," CNBC, June 5, 2017, https://www.cnbc.com/2017/06/02/what-this-ex-nsa-agent-wants-you-to-know-about-your-smartphone.html.
4. Robert O'Harrow Jr., "NSA Chief Asks a Skeptical Crowd of Hackers to Help Agency Do Its Job," *Washington Post*, July 31, 2013, https://www.washingtonpost.com/world/national-security/nsa-chief-asks-a-skeptical-crowd-of-hackers-to-help-agency-do-its-job.
5. Electronic Frontier Foundation, "NSA Spying: How it Works," https://www.eff.org/nsa-spying/how-it-works.

## Chapter 6: Joining the Team

1. NSA, "Resources for Students and Educators," https://www.nsa.gov/resources/students-educators.
2. NSA, "Careers," https://www.intelligencecareers.gov/NSA/nsacareers.html.
3. "National Security Agency Interview Questions," Glassdoor, https://www.glassdoor.com/Interview/National-Security-Agency-Interview-Questions-E41534_P3.htm.
4. USIC, "Application Process," Intelligence Careers, https://www.intelligencecareers.gov/icapply.html.
5. NSA Homepage, https://www.nsa.gov.

# GLOSSARY

**black hat** A hacker who breaks into other people's computers for nefarious or criminal reasons, such as when spies hack into the computers of other countries' intelligence agencies.

**cipher** A secret code used to create a message only certain people can read. A cipher is usually created using a mathematical formula to make it harder to break.

**cryptology** The study of codes and coded messages.

**cybersecurity** The process of protecting all electronic devices and messaging systems. Cybersecurity is what keeps emails, text messages, and computer programs safe from hackers and viruses.

**Department of Defense** The main government agency that oversees many of the intelligence agencies. The Department of Defense, or DOD, is responsible for overseeing all of the United States' national security measures and war-fighting operations, including cybersecurity.

**encryption** When a message is coded and locked so that only the sender and recipient can read the content, even if a third party is able to get a copy of the message.

**hacker** Someone who uses secret methods of gaining access to another person's or country's computers or electronic messages without that person or country knowing. Some hackers do this to help point out security flaws, while others do it to steal information or cause trouble for the entity being hacked.

**HUMINT** Human intelligence, or information gathered from talking to people and gaining insights into the knowledge they have.

**intelligence agency** A government agency responsible for gathering and analyzing information in order to protect the country's national security interests.

**intercept** To gain access to a message after it has been sent but before it reaches the recipient. Intelligence agencies often try to intercept messages shared between terrorists or other governments in order to gain insight into their private thoughts and actions.

**quantum computer** A super computer that is capable of cracking codes because it can focus on only the one code and works incredibly fast.

**September 11** The worst terror attack on the United States occurred on September 11, 2001; often shortened to September 11, or 9/11. This is the date when most intelligence agencies changed how they work because of the failures that occurred that allowed terrorists to attack the country on that day.

**SIGINT** Signals intelligence, or information gathered from electronic signaling devices, such as satellites, radar systems, communications systems, or weapons targeting systems.

**white hat** A hacker who works to help people and agencies that it hacks by finding security flaws in digital systems and pointing them out so that the system can be repaired before a black hat hacker can find the vulnerability.

# FURTHER READING

## Books

Harper, Allen, et al. *Gray Hat Hacking: The Ethical Hacker's Handbook, Fifth Edition*. New York, NY: McGraw-Hill Education, 2018.

Kaplan, Fred. *Dark Territory: The Secret History of Cyber War*. New York, NY: Simon & Schuster, 2016.

Ronczkowski, Michael R. *Terrorism and Organized Hate Crime: Intelligence Gathering, Analysis, and Investigations*. Boca Raton, FL: CRC Press, 2018.

Sanger, David E. *The Perfect Weapon: War, Sabotage, and Fear in the Cyber Age*. New York, NY: Crown Publishing, 2018.

Schneier, Bruce. *Data and Goliath: The Hidden Battles to Collect Your Data and Control Your World*. New York, NY: W.W. Norton & Company, 2015.

## Websites

**National Security Agency**
*www.nsa.gov*
The official site of the NSA features information about the history and activities of the agency, employment opportunities within the agency, and news and updates about the NSA and the state of cybersecurity around the world.

**The NSA Files by *The Guardian***
*www.theguardian.com/us-news/the-nsa-files*
*The Guardian* newspaper's web page devoted to the documents leaked by Edward Snowden. The website has articles about and analyses of the leaked documents, as well as deeper stories about the NSA and how it operates, all written by professional journalists and subject-matter experts.